The What of Underfoot

poems by

Julia Blumenreich

Finishing Line Press
Georgetown, Kentucky

The What of Underfoot

For Drew

Copyright © 2021 by Julia Blumenreich
ISBN 978-1-64662-649-6 First Edition
All rights reserved under International and Pan-American Copyright Conventions. No part of this book may be reproduced in any manner whatsoever without written permission from the publisher, except in the case of brief quotations embodied in critical articles and reviews.

ACKNOWLEDGMENTS

Thank you to Leonard Gontarek and The Osage Poets Group where many of these poems were first workshopped.

Publisher: Leah Huete de Maines
Editor: Christen Kincaid
Cover Art: Wendy Osterwell, www.wendyosterwell.com
Author Photo: Andrew Miller
Cover Design: Elizabeth Maines McCleavy

Order online: www.finishinglinepress.com
also available on amazon.com

Author inquiries and mail orders:
Finishing Line Press
PO Box 1626
Georgetown, Kentucky 40324
USA

Table of Contents

Ordinary 1

After School 2

River 3

How 4

A True Story 5

Full Bowl 6

The 5:30 7

Gone is not to sleep 8

I'll go on 9

Mute Swan 10

Two Years Spring 11

2:30am 12

Overheard 13

On the way to Pastorious Park 14

Now 15

Untitled 17

Dedication 18

Granma Hilda and Joseph Brodsky 20

Small talk 21

How I was a Mongolian orphan and an extraterrestrial
   in one life 22

My poetry teacher bought my painting my brother took
   his life 23

The Only Harmless Great Thing 24

Armchair Travelers' Checklist 25

Lewis Carroll and the Ghost 27

First Person 29

Meditation at 25 30

On Lilacs and Other Things 31

> "There is nothing you can see that is not a flower;
> there is nothing you can think that is not the moon."
> —Matsuo Basho

Ordinary

To learn something new the path you took yesterday, take that,
pledge yourself to familiarity
in routine in constancy there's a vitality
kiss me once, twice, three times before bed.
Look around the waiting room appreciate the tabloids currency the one patient
whose leg won't stop shaking reading gloss until he's called.
Worrying the spirea and roses your neighbor describes her son's
kindergarten asking for more than the loud impress of the teacher's personality
resolving to listen become quite typical in the stunning late Autumn afternoon.

Gather then in the cathedral of mahogany leaves ablaze in the outside end of beauty exclamation marks around the mouth graying brows eyelids shedding leaves and hair.

In this season of mounting darkness I am no wiser than decades ago over what we do to each other. Let's flock to the scenic route for a few weeks this fall. Take my hand, then, bring me closer that's all

After School

Today I want to talk to the geese.
Ask them why they're only four
whether I'm looking for meaning in the wrong place.

The late afternoon sky this February is all wooly hanging into the landscape
it's taking forever to leave this all behind.

This lifetime of exclamations as I cross the parking lot
geese honk from behind to encourage speed up front
I want them to be outraged over our President
mixing up the Japanese Prime Minister with the South Korean
for using 4th grade superlatives like tremendous and stupendous
ignoring the warming lake circumventing migration.

What if even when I die
what they say to each other remains a secret?
If all I should have cared about was how
the upwash of the goose ahead supports the bird behind
lifting it beyond its own strength.

Here's when my arms raise over my head
not in surrender but imagining our brief conversation
as a lifting out of myself.

I might be getting closer to reading Buddhist texts
or Wittgenstein about consciousness
as right now I'm the shawl of sky
the geese move through.

River
for the Children of Sandy Hook Elementary School

This is the place the place where words wash away
instinctually each syllable, each syllable floats near the others.
The torn-apart vowel or consonant sounds lost, the left
wing of the fledgling separated, the left wing from its right partner
never to sing for the sake of sun, or for the world below to call out
with recognition, recognition on its tongue like honey. Instead
wrenched open over river rocks, raw umber, burnt sienna, red clay
now only letters, these letters once were the names
the names of twenty children.
How could the "J" for "Jack" or the two "i"s in "Olivia," the quiet "h" at
"Noah's" end, say enough, say the life of those now dead?
This place, this place where the words once were flesh and blood
how their very hearts were swallowed.
Who can make sense, these letters that are left floating on the surface
unattached, cold, no longer their names.

How

I want to put in this poem the sun this morning presenting the clouds as segments of river clay rolled deliberately into slabs.

The light rails silent though trains must have already gone by.
The silhouettes of unidentifiable wings   who am I to think they're going somewhere?

It rises a poem the bread you used to whack down in celebration of its wildness
the dish towel a blanket repeatedly letting go.

We remember February as a painting entered with the cold smelled in the baking left. Breath comes out silver, silver sun, silver sky, silver cuts with blades.

As if the landscape were a map of where to go   silence discovered the artist saying
these are the steps that keep you here.

In the distance someone works to clear it's the first time I'm not afraid.

Day and night there is a chance to find where I'm going.
So many now have shed their coats in their task the snow falling surrounding my waist

They have made a space.   So much imagined I am confused.

Maybe going inside this frozen world alive   bucks and young mothers sharing this space.

A True Story

At the start of winter a woman cupped her face turning towards
the train's window
words foreground to all the trees she'll never see again

accusations, allegations, allegiances
enveloping the light an empty landscape cutting through
this movement.

Let's act like it doesn't matter if the president is sane. "*Little Rocket Man*" isn't a graphic novel 10-year-olds read. Let's override the truth like this president

flaunting the ultimate privilege.

If it's a "*so what because we must*" elect a predator with a predilection for young girls
then her father's father never burned his beloved stuffed puppy or disowned his children countless times.
Colony Collapse Disorder isn't a signal of an impending threat
nor is the frequency of natural disasters. The Holstein waiting in the chute to be killed
would say out loud "this is my purpose" its terrified eyes inconsequential.

Even the sloth has emotions, needs movement in order to live healthfully
"animal" comes from *anima* meaning "soul" as well as movement
she tells herself if she looks out the train window long enough she will be the window
the pines will turn lilac-gray when it snows
her father didn't really mean he'd murder her before his suicide
the former president had to learn not to cry as he comforted the living.

Full Bowl

Azaleas at dusk just after the scorch of sun
before they fade, background light of evening.
A child throws herself on the big world of pavement
counting each part of a ladybug, *does it have a heart?*

The setting is not an end but carries our future inside its ever-present
carries what we know of the world, it's wine spilled last night, the
peonies in their
decadence pouring over the circle of the graying vase, caught
in impermanence
before their petals will release in the over bounty.

The brushstrokes that evoke the light, white and wide with desire.
This whole world wants to enter that jab of color swallowing change
with its insistent longing.
Let us into this way of seeing, convey what we can only observe.
Know that something happens outside the frame, the blue door we
cannot enter
   if we could we might never have to leave, full bowl on the table.

The 5:30

This is one life. Reply you know.
Say this means so much great blue heron
maple leaves in the Wissahickon mattress
no longer on the floor. My one life is here
roving with others on the way to you. Tell me
you know it's a night for warm cider place
your coat on the radiator so good to see you
how was the station? Say you felt my footsteps
arriving with all the bundling
the waiting area crowded geese
descending on crumbs.

Wonder why it has to be like this   travelers an ocean
surging onto an escalator its trudge unable to do anything
shoving us back underwater to wait and wait. Say you could've
called your voice would've found a way through the tunnel
this place we go sometimes where the gorge reaches down to pat
the creek's shoulders when it's lonely. Here in this one life royal fern
red fox umbrella magnolia and tulip poplar a leaf refusing release
say settle here this ground between.

Corridor one swale between two hills
whose arm is around my shoulders?
Heft of bags and cases clipped wings
looking watching each other and not
my life is on some lace widening taking
the stairway down.

Gone is not to sleep

Scooping them up I crumbled thinking *who throws away the hole you made?*
Clouds all over the living room floor rain goddammit rain.
I hate the heavy curtains drawn see me now walk over slide them open trying to turn this paper over together we'd pretend you were unreachable
you'd never let go.
Who died and made you the boss of me?
Every time I leave a room I try to turn off the lights is this just a bad joke the way
we are taught to go dark.
Opposites infest me the fact it's night in that other hemisphere my body tilting towards. The moon spiraling inward, helpful gravity can rip away
one to become another, as in icy remnants of the bygone
what we see today.

I'll go on

Clear days, memory as weather. The old couple
took us up the coast. We could see a thousand small fires in another
country.

We drank coffee from porcelain cups, night stirring away.
Who knew then that we should memorize the wrinkled backs
of their hands

staring into somewhere else. The woman's white hair, the man's
slight limp.
They're here so I can think the thoughts that only occur when
you've rid yourself

of who you thought you were. Those were actually fireflies.
We spilled the contents
of our jars, our pockets until everyone laughed as they singed
the blackness.

Being young it's about summer wearing on. Even that did not seem
that unusual, clean linen on the side yard line, indenting the longest
day of the year. The light held there

was just another bonfire. Our lives are made up of stories which might
as well be true
those dead who make us say their names. Every time dug down
to something unsettling.

My eyes see your blue eyes waiting for me, lifting the wildflowers
from their beds
staring into their faces. Your head on two pillows propped up
by a nurse.

We opened our fists and let's not pretend why I had a key,
 or when the sonnet was memorized. *I can't go on, I'll go on.*

Mute Swan

mate for life dying of heartbreak after a partner goes eight foot wingspan unfolding
folding oneself into another is risky a friend said stirring a coffee
what if this is more than is bearable close the fold and crease
say a prayer that all my kindnesses will be remembered by the mute swans the canal
I wish I lived by.

Fold means so much the dog-eared pages I turn down as I read looking for words to chant I don't use a pen when it is over I find words strung together endlessly white lights the constellation of Cygnus viewable this time of year.

Look at a child a book of kites miracle of origami unfolding flying away the book won't close until the child catches and folds into himself
the leavings
the man who reaches up in the Linden places the wet-winged painted lady
on the budding branch sees it joined quickly by another in the music of wing-beats and color unfolding.

At four and one half months flying lessons begin their tiny wings hinged in the unfolding
the kiss of the female or pen as the cygnets lift off her back this life this very good life
in ways I am folded by you into a crease of cotton t-shirts with light pressure holding it still   into a fortune teller spread like a rumor through my fourth graders its names
and predictions of children in the folds   the thousand cranes before we die
the only way to refold the tape-strewn map the trick in the stack of folded fitted sheets
the swishing created by the wings of a mute swan in flight can be heard a mile away each wing a page widowed by words we follow how their shadows fold up and down back into the night.

Two Years Spring

Here are the flat faces sunbathing pink and white dogwoods
where the road cuts between house stories
fist-sized red and yellow tulips line their drive turn orange

Redbud flowers generous
Here is where the house must have risen.

Here, branches my arms, wrists and fingers let me turn tissue thin
catch in her magenta offerings. Toss eggs each night at the beast.

Planeless blue plate sky we look away from each other cross the road

Here, painted inside our eyelids are the lonely ones, a drive-in screen
with face after face.

At this age who hasn't thought about dying?
Or fancied for 24 hours a safe sky?

Like this year, a wet spring.
Deck bundled with annuals
garden climbing and announcing.

The shower and the week before the wedding poured. No matter
you both were radiant, the pandemic months away.

Back then, everyone held the hands of their loved ones when they left.

2:30am

Promise me the translation of cat's calls
one day the robin and her fledglings were gone
bird shit splattered rosebush
milkweed heads look right through the morning
a snapping turtle could take a few toes off.

It's cold sweat scrunched into a ball
3 baby birds with their mouths wide open
the dog panicking at the sudden deluge is inconsolable
see it's not all about me.

Churning stomach   red-tailed hawk
talons leave scars
none of the mantras are working
peaceful at ease like worms collected at recess.

The cardinal's head beneath the rosebush
her nest in shambles babies swallowed
a year later starving as the lightening begins
eggshells in the compost.

Counting the days she loves me he loves me
in the nature nook an antennaed slug in the dirt soup
paperwork and pebble collections
feathers suffering my side of the bed.

Overheard

Notice what all the blue-black butterflies edged in cornflower said
as they tried to stop me from putting the words on their wings.

We're talking secrets here now that I've gotten old enough
to think about dying without knowing yours or you mine.

Instead of reading daily editorials there's my horoscope and tarot
finding veracity in the breakfast light silent sun.

Some of the fantasies might be ok to show you
an anonymous angel placed in the nearest doorway willing
to be grandly bored
shown little gratitude when preventing four car pile-ups shattered
wrists and ankles.

What child hasn't imagined wings jumping off a sagging mattress
between elbow-flaps?
Wanting to be Ruler of the World or Tinkerbell
granting wishes and wisdom when the news from away is horrifying.

Ice cream jingle when I should be listening to what's wrong
with this country
walking by red gladiolas triggers the dystopian series so I turn
to the purple
the underside of tongues, a transplanted heart.

On the way to Pastorious Park

walking apart from a stranger
shoving masks around
our necks. Not to be
in step with intimacy as it
isn't written that way. Instead it's
something else, the legs failing to listen
my eyes trying the leafed distance, my heart
knows this space. Whole body gives
its opinion as we are now points on a line
in step with each other, arrows
at each end. For this moment
there is no exhale
dying again from otherness.
Let me look into the what
of underfoot.

Now

-1-

We really do need to know what we want
the situation in this country
after all untenable, which we try to hold.

-2-

It turns out that hunger isn't the only reason that life breaks apart
the petals on the lilies too long in the vase
but odd now to know such a thing.

-3-

How can I tell which of us is absent?
A set of streetlamps extinguished by one
what our responses should be or are.

-4-

Reacting with shock my mind went on and said too much
I cannot see to see
but such happens to me.

-5-

When can we disregard the course of these events?
maybe a long time
I've been all *wrapped up in my bits and pieces.*

-6-

This is an instance of the world
meaning to leave myself open
a moth in a jar, once caterpillar.

Untitled

> *No one would know anything more about me, a woman trying*
> *to re read re connect re member*
> *black/white/other*
> *it's a lily pad of identity*
> *—Anonymous woman*
> *(written long ago on a napkin placed in a notebook)*

The sentence begins: "If I were to die right now…?" Peeling skin
of answers to letters
to be so old as to disappear before my cupped hands. If I dig too
violently the unearthing avoids grasping rather I know she feels much
more than
her crossed arms
mean. Maybe at the bottom when the collections are given to paper
bug wings occasional electric currents. Filthy blank books.

Was she changed by an act of violence knowing it was coming someday?
Her house hadn't burned but the words she wanted to have me find
choked me in rage
in loss. A whole city of stories left burning with a full head of stars
or worse scattered
everywhere in the way her eyebrow wouldn't grow back her legs
walked maligned by veins. Her sex stalled. broken.

Perhaps this is for that *wild* woman
with electrified hair metaphor and alliteration
who when I'm writing and later when you're reading this
or when I'm reading this again to see her being beaten before you
or I could help
to see if I can name her.

Remember she tried to cross
space culture time and myth
with a page that could hold her form
if only for a moment before
dissolving with the air.

I can prove none of this
yet a poem later
she exists.

Dedication
    "A fairy tale is not an allegory" —George MacDonald

Mama Simon places the two watches she wears
on the console
they do not agree on the time.

Pushing their faces together she listens
between the points they don't touch on.
She is trying to figure out which one to believe.

                *

When tomorrow two heads knock together, running to her
with their lives passing before them. "What you said
yesterday, we will help   you are right."

                *

Mama Simon clacks the word, fat beads of clover flowers and eggshells
rise off her chest. Over her entire lawn lie rectangles of brick, not one
blade
of grass whistling up through the mortar. She cuts diagonally
to the first

morning person, who shakes his head, not doing well
with what she says.
She tries another, placing her lips around the words as if they were
somewhere else.
He only hugs her, his arms cross and stick out straight.

Behind him her tree stump from where she plans
her best strategies, along with letters
to Senators, conglomerates, chiefs and astronauts.

                *

Tied at the market, a dog hears voices. "But the babies," she tries two
sisters passing much later. They aren't stopping   aren't looking back.
The mongrel lifts his leg
on the concrete, petting him he wags close to her   their forms evaporate
in no light.

*

Now quiet   then not. Before she disappears, the yard hosed down
a basin filled. Pluto barks once   leaves her.
Around petitions she wipes her open hands.

*

Mama Simon looks up from her gardening, uprooted bricks hiding
under her full skirt.
Unruffled, she knocks out reasons, pouring years and what to call
the future
evenly into four outstretched hands.

What more do you want than this life I build?

Granma Hilda and Joseph Brodsky

My five black dresses swept stars
yes we have dwelt here
sometimes I disappear with them in the bedroom closet

Leave our names alone don't construct those vowels, consonants
and so forth
ourselves   utter garbage, swine, refujew
I couldn't wait for the horses made monsters by their riders
my two hands made one
The bulb looks at the flower in fear

What's fertile falls in fallow soil
I am the leaf departing without goodbye.

The hunger we devoured without tasting
wasting those delicious things come walking
I look where breath beats underwater once they belonged wild to me
my country the plow of my back breaking the surface outwitting
my song was out of tune, my voice cracked
but at least no chorus can ever sing it back

I wonder if anyone can see the black hole too close to my heart
I always wore a dress   I leaned my hips   watched
for land   not yet a tragic figure
we toast our shoes tongues over waves until we can see the deck
from above

See how it follows me
my black dress a ship
In America *I sit in the dark*
hear roaches mothers and children
in corners letting them live.

Small talk

Aren't they having fun? Swallowtails flying near then away from each other.
Brown ducks sitting creek side, not from around here, maybe they're talking
in their not. I find it so much easier to think about conversing with them than with most people. Don't call me antisocial, it has more to do with understanding so I ask too many questions. *Stop interviewing me.* One goddamn thing I know is there have been moments when the lines of poetry just came through me, dinging all my senses on the way to the page, my body pressed up against a pinball machine shaking the words out. The only time I know what I want to say is when I've written about death. One little two little three little losses. My brother's small hands folded by the mortician, my late husband's elegant fingers looped through an angel. I admit the story I tell myself isn't true, but it's what I got besides some voice that makes me describe my Russian tortoise's eyes as bored, its closed mouth leaning into obscenities with the lights on. Lilacs kindled through the breakfast room where my parents dined on bread pyramids suspended over a moat of egg yolks, except there was no such room, just a grease pencil image on a lithography stone. Innocent at five when my mother slapped me watching cartoons, leaving marks. In the photo at ten sitting on the edge of my father's chair, my eyes know no one taught me how to love: turn the soil over, dig a gaping mouth with the trowel, center the tight-fisted impatiens, blanket them and tuck them in, and water, water, water.

How I was a Mongolian orphan and an extraterrestrial in one life

Everyone lied. The dog was gone to the farm when I came home from school
There were orange shit lilies growing where the cows backed up to the fence.
I would've been the only Jewish kid in Fargo, North Dakota so my father ditched
the transfer and moved us to the PA suburbs. The real reason he started over
he stole from Bulova Watch Company. He gambled our money burning through it oregano joints smoked in the attic.

My mother loved her friends more than me. She made up stories. I was certainly adopted from Mongolia except I resembled my father.
On the phone my mother told her friends my college boyfriend looked like Jesus.
Then she denied it all.   I started communing with extraterrestrials so alienated did I feel.
Instead of a stork bringing me I imagined a space ship dropping me in the middle of a hot smoky poker game. The chips fanning around me hard and rough.
"Get this baby the fuck outta here; get off the phone!" My mother didn't hang up. My father kept playing. My brother 11 years older watched my birth: *You were a miracle. You saved me.* Decades later my brother gambled everything away becoming the father we hated. One morning
my sister-in-law called   my brother blew his brains out.
The air was warmer in Dallas than up in PA it was gray enough to ache all.

My poetry teacher bought my painting my brother took his life
after "Yellow Stars and Ice," by Susan Stewart

I am as far as the horseshoe nailed over the old barn door
and you are as far as my river mouth canvas
he is the brother who lassoed a gun to his head.

You are how we circled around you
covered wagons filled with night terrors and smoke
he is my brother who might after dark
suggest I gouge my thighs and forearms
I am as far as your horse, Sterling
as my memory scraped gravel deep from its hooves.

He is the one who wasn't hungry, drinking the bottle he held
to the light
leaving the label pressed to the bathroom mirror
you are the mother who read her three-year-old poems
and spoke of temporality, a frame as another year ends.
I am the one who thinks of you right before you appear on Forbidden
Drive
or leaving the Chinese restaurant as we sit down.

You are the one delighting in my thesis "Who's Who"
thinking I dreamt of Emily Dickinson
I am the one twenty years later who crumbled on the headmaster's rug
like I had any idea what to do.
He is the one who locked the bathroom door
never reading a single one of my poems
never showing them to him
black and white warblers lost their way.

The Only Harmless Great Thing

In the elephant graveyard, we scattered my brother's bones
the largest land animals look after the wounded, the bones of the dead.

Born wearing wrinkles
noses have fingers
they wave hello with their ears
talk in deafening rumbles
move around on soundless feet
like us.

Poachers on horseback carrying AK47s and machetes for tusks
he knew he would die, they didn't

there's the cloudless sky
mothers and their calves feel them coming
they know the towardness of death
the cloudlessness tears through the paper-thin day
gunshots to the skull
is this what the mortician saw before he reconstructed his face?

Thou shalt not kill elephants
We wrote with a stick on the forest floor.

It would be murder to shoot the elephant.
It would be murder to shoot oneself.

Armchair Travelers' Checklist

Consider arranging for the post office to hold your mail
or have someone collect it for you daily.

Dear Spirit:

O life
O beyond life O other side

Ask if they will take care of animals, plants; separate the trash
from the recycling. Leave a key with the person you trust.

I let you go
and you moved as a cloud of bees to universe land

Just in case, arrange for travelers' contingency insurance.
Tag luggage with brightly colored lanyards and whistles.
Pack extra medications and prescriptions; you might be delayed. Go ahead, leave a light on.

me tell you didn't Why
O that's where I'd find you.
Try and try
who would think you'd be in
the sweet smelling bowl of transplanted acorns and crunchy oak leaves?

Bring names, addresses, and phone numbers of people to contact in an
emergency. Currency of the country and some cash.

Vast is the maze
too small to see over the sides
the uncertainty is physical
a desert landscape
labyrinth, a dream
of flapping and floating over the possible.

*The question is does landing
in this world
a dot squeezed in
if you really look
make for unexpected interruptions?*

Empty refrigerator and turn it to a low setting. Leave the garden spigot with a slow drip.
Lock all doors and windows.
Sprinkle fresh mint for luck.

*This art of walking
takes time takes
thinking just the right amount to smooth voluntary to involuntary.*

Takes the blood pulsing the muscles and the joints hinging like a door to the cellar.

*A form mobile as seen
from the end of a lengthy lichen-colored corridor
would be faceless
if not for you.
Your indomitable back,
the weightless prints sprinkled by the back door
announcing: "I am
the purveyor of my soul!"*

*Ice cold evening
your ashes thrown
for all the oceans and suns. I see you walking
before you left by boat. Your scented fingers relaxing out into the water.*

Lewis Carroll and the Ghost

Knowing things is sometimes trouble. One report led me to his ghost. He
hop-hurries somewhere around the house talking to himself who knows

what he's doing half the time. I have learned to call him Charles
Charles, I'm home, is what I forget to say.

I've stopped cooking him dinner because he doesn't eat
though at times I still set a place for him.

I want to ask him about his day but I don't and later
when I'm researching his extinction I know he's there silently

egging me on. But what am I to do with him when I can't see him? He
is almost like my late husband and my brother here than just nowhere
not even ghosts.

I try a different tactic with Charles.
Aren't you yet afraid of humans?

Those Dutch sailors were one reason you vanished from Mauritius
their own hunt of you as easy as inviting you for tea.

His voice appears while I sleep: *I'm not mythical but a symbol*
of obsolescence
I'm here with my fears of loneliness and being forgotten again.

Random words in window wells. Impotent wings proof it's a bird
Fat-arse. Melancholic visage. Dodo DNA rumored at Oxford.

That's trouble.   You've already gone too far making me believe
you're here.
I can't be good enough introducing you into the ecosystem again.

Might be too much of a disappointment might turn out to be just like other birds.

Don't you know my story? He answers. *Come let's run a race in any pattern and shape starting and ending whenever we like.*
So everyone wins.

First Person

So all the plans had changed, no sound sparkling below, billowing.
When you could see it through the rain, the landscape was gray, unrelenting.

Inside, the kind of pleasant confusion you don't forget
stringing out its intricate possibilities. A good day for escape.

Some books are better than others, I say it loudly but only the sleeping dog responds.
I say it into the shelves lined with theory. I say it to the vocabulary ignoring meaning.

Some books are damp from exertion, some survived never being opened at all.
They are all haunted by water.   I am haunted by what I can't escape.

The singular cry. We could name them, brave voices standing out from the crowd. But we wouldn't agree. Though we are looking

for the same: *someone was here before me, someone felt this, some one.*

Meditation at Twenty-Five

What of it stones that beat sheets white heels
smooth. What we do according
to the teachings of another.

Who gets through that time of day the exhausting light
photos never hung the wanting walls.

Ferocious and infused a head turns with this
crackles on top of the spine   falls.

The recipe was passed down and she uses extra ginger cause she feels like it.
She could be thinking about fussing and comparing but says
"nothing really."

The legend goes the fortune is coming some day.
She really is quite lucky when she gives it a shot.

Didn't make it on "The Price is Right" she keeps the t.v. off
watches the crystal ball of the screen.

"Dunno, just can't answer such things" the bread is rising.

Hot crumbs coat the knife that's how you tell if the dough is cooked.
The oven can't be trusted it's getting awfully late.

Someone is telling the story again. In the portioned light she sits pretends to listen.
It's never been so quiet there at the square the plaza the center.

On Lilacs and Other Things

    Upturned to the sun
To love the whole body like it belongs.

    What if I spoke as I wrote
A translation please!

    Getting away with murder
stealing bushels of chances.

    Accept all
Except trespassers.

    A superball might go to heaven tick-tock
As children endlessly.

    Lilacs whistle indecently
"I know you" seems to say.

    We're at furiously now the past is the dance.
Is the dance we're at furiously now the ?

    Who runs the race & then she said to remind me
"While we all die with nothing to hide there is little I have told you."

Julia Blumenreich is a poet who is in her 25th year of teaching 4th grade at Germantown Academy in Fort Washington, PA. She is a recipient of a Pennsylvania Arts Council grant for her poetry and a finalist for the 2016 Brittany Noakes Poetry Award. She has read her work in various venues including the University of Pennsylvania, Brown University, and Muse House in Philadelphia. In 2012, she collaborated with the visual artist, Wendy Osterweil, on 'Reforesting: An Homage to Gil Ott' a poetry/ sculptural installation/print show at The Painted Bride Art Center. Four of her poems have been set to music composed by Kyle Smith and were performed as part of "Lyric Fest" in 2014. Her recent work has been published in "The Whirlwind Review, "Philadelphia Stories," and in "An Anthology of Philadelphia Poets," edited by Valerie Fox and translated into Romanian by Daniel Dragomirescu. She has published three chapbooks: *Meeting Tessie* (Singing Horse Press), *Artificial Memory* (Leave Books) and *Blue Angel of a Day* (Moonstone Press).

www.ingramcontent.com/pod-product-compliance
Lightning Source LLC
LaVergne TN
LVHW041504070426
835507LV00012B/1316